Lerner SPORTS

ALL-STAR SMACKDOWN

SHOHEI OHTANI VS. DAVID ORTIZ

WHO WOULD WIN?

PETER DOUGLAS

Lerner Publications ◆ Minneapolis

The stats and information in this book are accurate through April 2025.

Lerner Publications Company
An imprint of Lerner Publishing Group, Inc.
241 First Avenue North
Minneapolis, MN 55401 USA

For reading levels and more information, look up this title at www.lernerbooks.com.

Main body text set in Aptifer Sans LT Pro.
Typeface provided by Linotype AG.

Library of Congress Cataloging-in-Publication Data

Names: Douglas, Peter, 1968–author
Title: Shohei Ohtani vs. David Ortiz : who would win? / Peter Douglas.
Other titles: Shohei Ohtani versus David Ortiz
Description: Minneapolis, MN : Lerner Publications, [2026] | Series: All-star smackdown (Lerner sports) | Includes bibliographical references and index. | Audience: Ages 7–11 | Audience: Grades 2–3 | Summary: "Shohei Ohtani and David Ortiz are both all-time great baseball players. But who would win in a head-to-head matchup? Read about exciting highlights, uncover key stats, and decide for yourself who takes the crown"—Provided by publisher.
Identifiers: LCCN 2025011517 (print) | LCCN 2025011518 (ebook) | ISBN 9798765689486 library binding | ISBN 9798348028428 paperback | ISBN 9798765694466 epub
Subjects: LCSH: Ohtani, Shohei, 1994-—Juvenile literature | Baseball players—Japan—Biography—Juvenile literature | Pitchers (Baseball)—United States—Biography—Juvenile literature | Los Angeles Angels of Anaheim (Baseball team)—Juvenile literature | Ortiz, David, 1975-—Juvenile literature | Baseball players—Dominican Republic—Biography—Juvenile literature | Designated hitters (Baseball)—United States—Biography—Juvenile literature | Boston Red Sox (Baseball team)—Juvenile literature | LCGFT: Biographies
Classification: LCC GV865.A1 D66 2026 (print) | LCC GV865.A1 (ebook) | DDC 796.357092/2 [B]—dc23/eng/20250510

LC record available at https://lccn.loc.gov/2025011517
LC ebook record available at https://lccn.loc.gov/2025011518

Manufactured in the United States of America
2-1014410-54816-4/28/2026

TABLE OF CONTENTS

David Ortiz

INTRODUCTION

BIG HITTER BATTLE

It was Game 5 of the 2004 American League Championship Series. Going into the eighth inning, the Boston Red Sox were down 4–2

FAST FACTS

- Shohei Ohtani led the American League in home runs in 2023 and the National League in home runs in 2024.
- In 2024, Ohtani became the first player to ever hit 50 or more home runs and steal at least 50 bases in the same season.
- David Ortiz is an eight-time winner of the Edgar Martínez Award for best designated hitter.
- Ortiz hit 541 home runs in his 20 Major League Baseball (MLB) seasons.

to the New York Yankees. The Red Sox had lost three straight games to open the series. If New York won, Boston was out of the playoffs. That's when designated hitter David "Big Papi" Ortiz stepped up to the plate. He smashed a pitch deep into left field for a home run. The Red Sox scored another run, and the game stretched into the 14th inning.

Ortiz once again came up to bat. Boston's Johnny Damon waited eagerly on second base. Ortiz hit six foul balls before delivering a game-winning single to center field. Damon crossed home to score the winning run. The Red Sox went on to win the final two games in the series. They were the first MLB team in history to come back from being down three games to zero in a playoff series.

Shohei Ohtani

Almost 20 years later in 2023, Shohei Ohtani's Los Angeles Angels were getting ready to face off against the Detroit Tigers in a doubleheader. In the first game, Ohtani only gave up one hit as a pitcher. He struck out eight Tigers. Ohtani pitched the entire game. The Angels won 6–0 in a shutout.

In the second game, Ohtani made history by hitting two home runs. He had just become the second MLB player since 1900 to allow one hit or less as a pitcher and hit two home runs on the same day. The other was Rick Wise in 1971.

In 2004, Ortiz helped the Red Sox win the World Series for the first time in 86 years.

Ohtani looks on from the dugout during a 2023 doubleheader against the Detroit Tigers.

CHAPTER 1

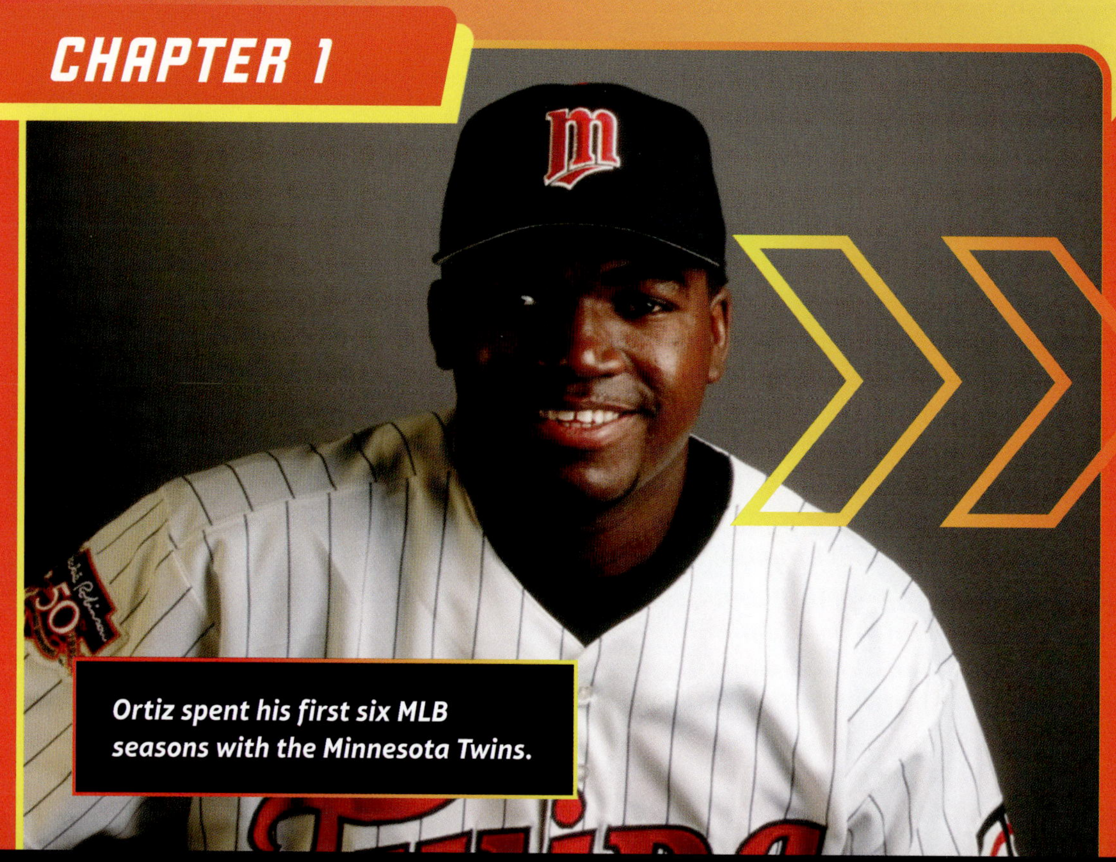

Ortiz spent his first six MLB seasons with the Minnesota Twins.

JOURNEY TO SUCCESS

David Ortiz was born in the Dominican Republic in 1975. Scouts noticed his skills from a young age, and he joined the Seattle Mariners in 1992 when he was only 17. Ortiz spent five years playing on farm teams to prepare him for the MLB. Even though he showed strong potential, the Mariners traded Ortiz to the Minnesota Twins in 1996. In 1997 for Minnesota's minor league teams, Ortiz had a batting average of .317 with 31 home runs and 124 RBIs (runs batted in).

Ortiz played in his first MLB game with the Twins on September 2, 1997. But he was sent down to the minor leagues many times over the next six seasons. He also struggled with injuries during his time in Minnesota.

The 2002 season would be Ortiz's last with the Twins. The Twins cut Ortiz in December. Early the next year, he signed with the Red Sox. After 10 long years in and out of the majors, he finally found success in Boston and went on to have a Hall of Fame career.

Ortiz runs the bases during a 2003 game against the New York Yankees.

Before Shohei Ohtani joined the MLB, he was already a baseball superstar in Japan. He played five seasons in Japan's Nippon Professional Baseball (NPB) league between 2013 and 2017. He was good at both hitting and pitching and liked to do both. But MLB teams told him he had to pick one if he wanted to play in North America.

Ohtani began his pro career at age 18. He was the first player to be drafted out of high school in Japan since 1951.

In his first season with the Angels, Ohtani hit 22 home runs, stole 10 bases, and struck out 63 hitters.

Ohtani led the NPB in ERA (earned run average) in 2015. In 2016, he was named the league's Most Valuable Player (MVP), and his team won the league championship. But Ohtani still dreamed of playing in the MLB someday. Several teams were interested. But the Los Angeles Angels agreed to let him pitch and hit. So at age 23, Ohtani left Japan for Los Angeles.

Ohtani soon began to dominate on his new team. He won the 2018 American League Rookie of the Year award. He won three MVP awards in his first seven seasons in the MLB. Six years later in 2024, Ohtani left the Angels and joined the Los Angeles Dodgers.

The Dodgers gave Ohtani a record-breaking $700 million contract to sign with them in 2023.

Ortiz gets ready to hit during the 2016 MLB All-Star game.

CONSIDER THIS

In his last MLB season, 40-year-old David Ortiz had a batting average of .315 with 38 home runs and a league-leading 127 RBIs.

CHAPTER 2

Ortiz takes a swing during a 2004 American League Division Series game against the Anaheim Angels.

GREAT MOMENTS

David Ortiz was known for getting a hit when his team really needed one. One example came during Boston's 2004 playoff series against the Anaheim Angels. Boston was up two games to none in the best of five series. If the Red Sox won, they would advance to the American League Championship Series. Game 3 was tied 6–6 in extra innings. Ortiz came to the plate with two outs. He stepped into the batter's box and blasted a home run into left field to win the game and the series.

In the next round of the playoffs, the Red Sox played the Yankees for a chance to go to the World Series. They got to play at their home stadium for Game 4, but they were already behind in the series three games to zero. The Yankees held the lead for much of the game. But a ninth inning single by Red Sox third baseman Bill Mueller tied the game 4–4.

Ortiz smiles after sending the Red Sox to the 2004 World Series.

Ortiz lifts the 2013 World Series trophy following a series-clinching Game 6 win.

The game was still tied going into the 12th inning. Again, it was Ortiz who came up with a clutch hit in a must-win situation. He hit another walk-off home run. Although it was a long shot, Ortiz gave Boston a chance to win the series. The Red Sox went on to win the World Series that season. It was the first World Series championship for Boston in 86 years.

In 2013, Boston was down 5–1 in the bottom of the eighth during a playoff game against the Detroit Tigers. Ortiz stepped up to bat with two outs and the bases loaded. He hit the very first pitch over the fence for a game-tying grand slam. Boston won the game 6–5. They completed the job by winning the series in six games to advance to the World Series.

CONSIDER THIS

In 2021, Shohei Ohtani was the first player to make the MLB All-Star Game as both a pitcher and position player. He pitched for one inning and did not allow a run.

On September 19, 2024, Shohei Ohtani was wrapping up a historic season. He entered the game against the Miami Marlins with 48 home runs and 49 stolen bases on the season. No player in MLB history had ever stolen 50 bases and hit 50 home runs in the same season. That night, Ohtani founded the 50/50 club in style.

Ohtani bats during his record-breaking 2024 game against the Miami Marlins.

Ohtani hit a career-high 54 home runs in 2024.

Ohtani got a hit all six times he was up to bat. He hit a double to start the game. Then Ohtani swiped third base for his 50th steal. In the next inning, Ohtani hit a single and stole second base for number 51. He still needed two home runs to make history.

In the sixth inning, Ohtani hit home run number 49. Then in the seventh, he sent the ball deep over the left field wall for his 50th home run. He hit one more home run later in the game. It also gave him 10 RBIs for the game. That was half of LA's total in the 20–4 win. The victory clinched a playoff spot for the Dodgers.

Another amazing night for Ohtani came in a regular-season game against the Chicago White Sox in June 2023. He threw 10 strikeouts and only allowed one run in just under seven innings. He also hit two home runs that night. The second came late in the game, after he was done pitching. It was a key hit in securing the 4–2 win.

On June 13, 2019, Ohtani hit a single, a double, a triple, and a home run in one game. This is called hitting for the cycle. Ohtani is the first Japanese-born player to ever hit for the cycle in an MLB game.

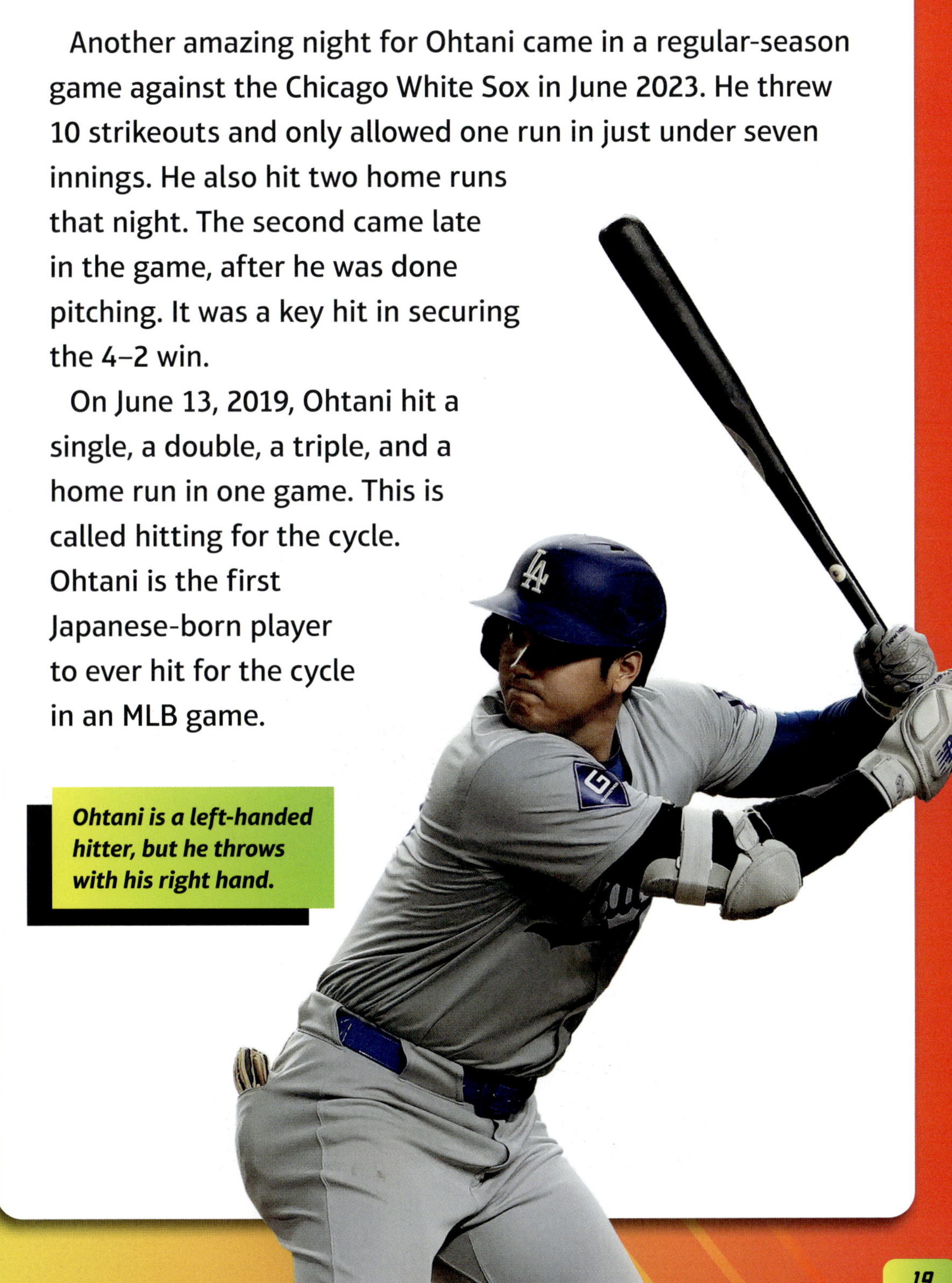

Ohtani is a left-handed hitter, but he throws with his right hand.

CHAPTER 3

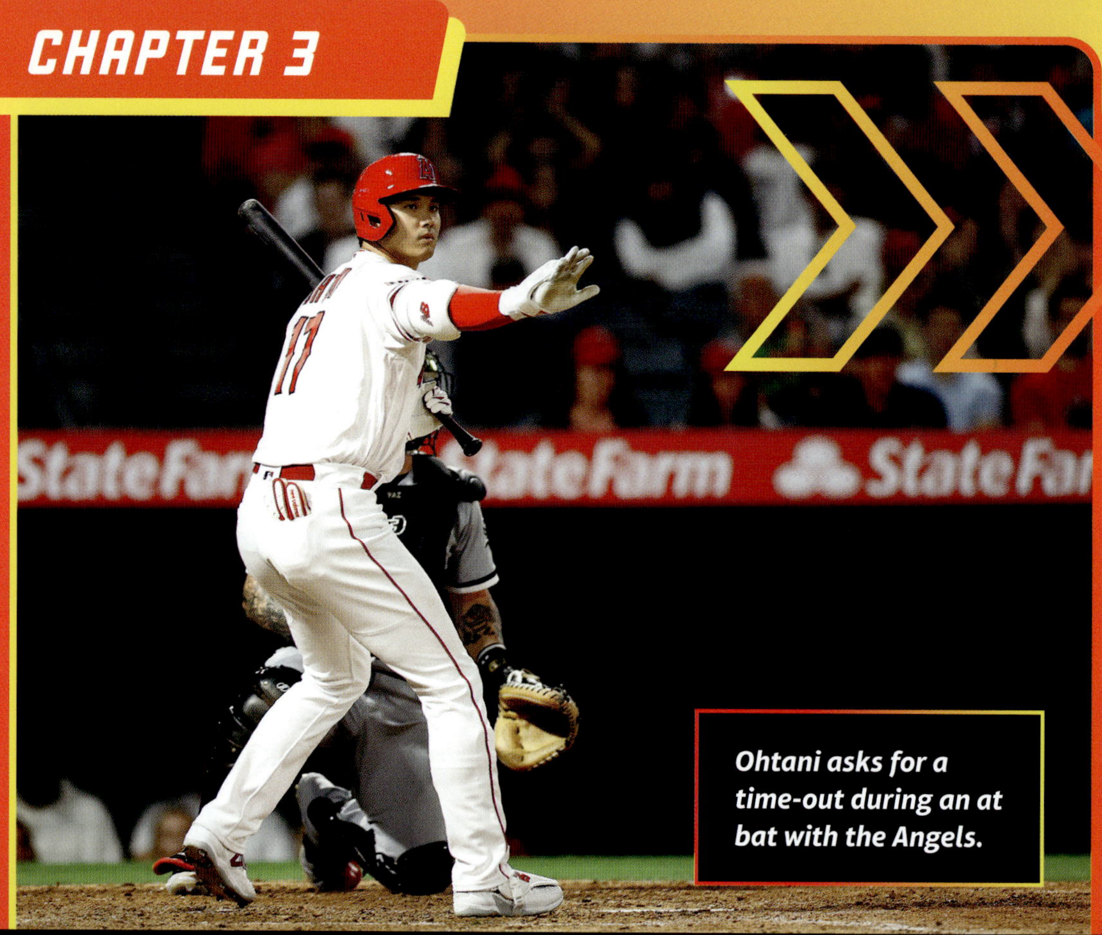

Ohtani asks for a time-out during an at bat with the Angels.

STAR SLUGGERS

Both Shohei Ohtani and David Ortiz are power hitters. Although they contribute in other ways, they are known for connecting on their powerful swings. They have each won the Edgar Martínez Award as the league's best designated hitter multiple times. Ortiz won it eight times, while Ohtani won it four years in a row from 2021 to 2024.

Ortiz was a great hitter in his Hall of Fame career. He hit 541 home runs in 20 seasons. That is 17th-most all-time. He also had 1,768 career RBIs. He led the MLB in RBI three times during his career. Ortiz is a career .286 hitter and went to 10 All-Star games.

Ortiz was a big part of three World Series titles. He was the World Series MVP in 2013 when he hit .688 in the series. Over his career, he hit 17 home runs and had 61 RBIs in the playoffs. Ortiz also has seven Silver Slugger Awards.

Ortiz returns to Boston's Fenway Park after being added to the Baseball Hall of Fame in 2022.

Ohtani tips his hat after receiving the 2022 Edgar Martínez Outstanding Designated Hitter Award at Angel Stadium.

At only 30 years old, Ohtani already has three MLB MVP awards. He led the American League in home runs in 2023 and did the same in the National League in 2024. He hit 44 in 2023 and 54 in 2024. Ohtani also stole 145 bases in his first seven MLB seasons. This makes him the career leader in

CONSIDER THIS

On September 19, 2024, Shohei Ohtani became the first member of the 50/50 club. That night, he also became the first player since 1901 with at least five extra-base hits and more than one stolen base in a game.

steals by a designated hitter. He is a career .282 hitter with 229 home runs and 572 RBIs. This has earned him three Silver Slugger Awards so far.

Ohtani is also an excellent pitcher. In 2022, he won 15 games and lost only nine for the Angels as a starting pitcher. Injuries kept him from pitching in 2019, most of 2020, and 2024. In the five seasons he did pitch, Ohtani was the starting pitcher in 86 games. His record was 38–19 with an ERA of 3.01.

Ohtani fires a pitch during a 2023 game against the Oakland Athletics.

CHAPTER 4

Ortiz's career took off when he joined the Red Sox.

AND THE WINNER IS

David Ortiz had a great career and is well-deserving of his spot in the Hall of Fame. He is one of the best clutch hitters of all time. But he never won a league MVP award. Ohtani has already earned that honor three times in his first seven seasons. Ortiz was just becoming a regular in the lineup with Boston at that point in his career.

Ortiz struggled to get to the majors. Ohtani has been dominant at every level in his career. He won Rookie of the Year in his first season with the Angels. Both Ortiz and Ohtani were great hitters. But Ohtani can pitch and steal bases as well.

Ohtani did not pitch in his first season with the Dodgers because of an injury in his elbow.

Based on Ohtani's career so far, it is hard to argue that he is not already a Hall of Famer. And he still has a long career ahead.

Shohei Ohtani is the clear winner of this smackdown. His ability to both hit and pitch at a high level is unmatched since the days of Babe Ruth 100 years ago. If he's being compared to Babe Ruth, it's clear that Ohtani is special.

Who do you think the winner is? Look at the facts and decide for yourself!

Ortiz was at his best in the playoffs. He batted .455 in 14 career World Series games.

With three MVPs, a Rookie of the Year award, a 50-plus HR season, and a .301 ERA so far, Ohtani is on track to be one of the greatest MLB players ever.

SMACKDOWN BREAKDOWN

SHOHEI OHTANI

Height: 6 feet 3 (1.91 m)
Career batting average: .282
Career ERA: 3.01
World Series championships: 1
League MVP awards: 3

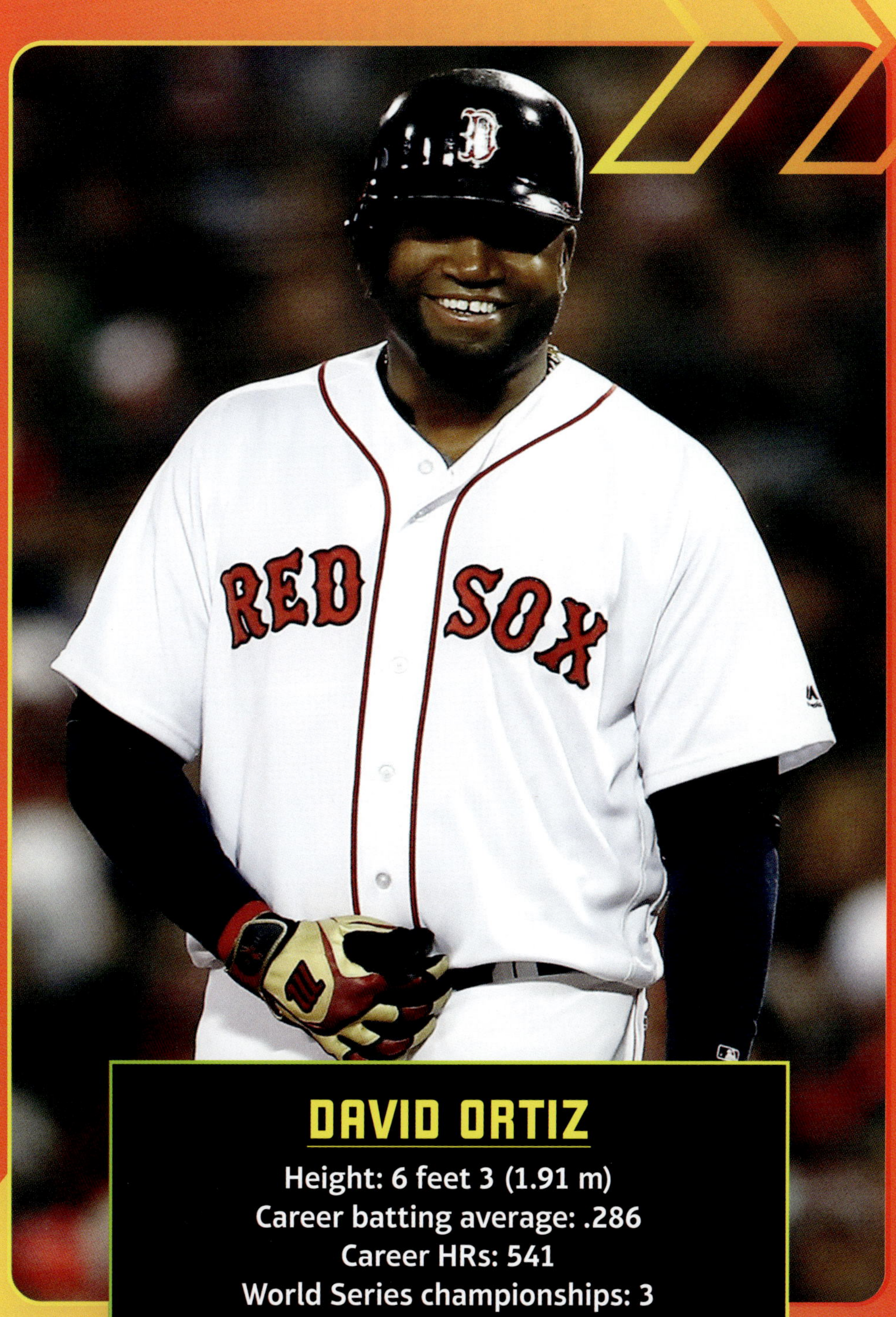

DAVID ORTIZ

Height: 6 feet 3 (1.91 m)
Career batting average: .286
Career HRs: 541
World Series championships: 3
League MVP awards: 0

GLOSSARY

batting average: a figure found by dividing the number of official times at bat into the number of base hits

designated hitter: the player who typically bats in place of the pitcher

doubleheader: two games played on the same day

earned run average (ERA): the average number of earned runs (runs scored without the benefit of an error) per game scored against a pitcher

grand slam: a home run that is hit with a runner on every base

home run: when a batter hits the ball out of the playing area between the foul poles

minor league: a pro baseball league where players develop their skills in an effort to advance to a major league team

RBI: short for run batted in, a run in baseball that is driven in by a batter

Silver Slugger: an award given to the player voted to be the best hitter at his position after each season

World Series: the final series in a season that determines that year's champion

LEARN MORE

Berglund, Bruce. *Baseball GOATs: The Greatest Athletes of All Time.* Capstone, 2022.

Britannica Kids: Shohei Ohtani
https://kids.britannica.com/students/article/Shohei-Ohtani/644641

Burrell, Dean. *Baseball Biographies for Kids: Stories of Baseball's Most Inspiring Players.* Callisto Kids, 2024.

Ducksters: Baseball
https://www.ducksters.com/sports/baseball.php

Ducksters: MLB
https://www.ducksters.com/sports/major_league_baseball.php

Fishman, Jon. *Shohei Ohtani.* Lerner Publications, 2022.

INDEX

PHOTO ACKNOWLEDGMENTS

Image credits: Doug Pensinger/Getty Images, p. 4; Duane Burleson/Getty Images, p. 5; Rich Pilling/MLB/Getty Images, p. 6; Mark Cunningham/MLB Photos/Getty Images, p. 7; Rick Stewart/Allsport/Getty Images, p. 8; Rick Stewart/Getty Images, p. 9; Atsushi Tomura/Getty Images, p. 10; Masterpress/Getty Images, p. 11; Rob Lester/MLB Photos, p. 12; Andy Hayt/Getty Images, p. 13; Al Bello/Getty Images, p. 14; Rob Leiter/MLB/Getty Images, p. 15; Jamie Squire/Getty Images, p. 16; Kelly Gavin/MLB Photos/Getty Images, p 17; Kelly Gavin/MLB Photos/Getty Images, p. 18; Jasen Vinlove/Miami Marlins/Getty Images, p. 19; Ronald Martinez/Getty Images, p. 20; Kathryn Riley/Getty Images, p. 21; John McCoy/Getty Images, p. 22; Suzanna Mitchell/MLB Photos/Getty Images, p. 23; Billie Weiss/Boston Red Sox/Getty Images, p. 24; Nuccio DiNuzzo/Getty Images, p. 25; Ron Vesely/MLB Photos, p. 26; Mary DiCicco/MLB Photos/Getty Images, p. 27; Justin Casterline/Getty Images, p. 28; Elsa/Getty Images, p. 29.

Cover: Brian Rothmuller/Icon Sportswire/Newscom; Lon Horwedel/Icon Sportswire/Newscom.